Spiritual Healing

An Innovative Approach
For Compassionate,
Effective Spiritual Health
And Healing

By

Megan Coulter

© Copyright 2015 by Megan Coulter - All rights reserved.

This publication is designed to provide accurate and authoritative information in regard to the subject matter covered. It is sold with the understanding that the publisher is not engaged in rendering legal, accounting or other professional services. If legal advice or other professional assistance is required, the services of a competent professional person should be sought.

- From a Declaration of Principles jointly adopted by a Committee of the American Bar Association and a Committee of Publishers and Associations.

All rights reserved. No part of this publication may be reproduced or transmitted in any form or by any means, electronic or mechanical, including photocopy, recording, or any information storage or retrieval system, without permission in writing from the publisher.

Spirituality

No responsibility or liability is assumed by the Publisher for any injury, damage or financial loss sustained to persons or property from the use of this information, personal or otherwise, either directly or indirectly. While every effort has been made to ensure reliability and accuracy of the information within, all liability, negligence or otherwise, from any use, misuse or abuse of the operation of any methods, strategies, instructions or ideas contained in the material herein, is the sole responsibility of the reader.

Any copyrights not held by publisher are owned by their respective authors.
All information is generalized, presented for informational purposes only and presented "as is" without warranty or guarantee of any kind.

All trademarks and brands referred to in this book are for illustrative purposes only, are the property of their respective owners and not affiliated with this publication in any way. Any trademarks are being used without permission, and the publication of the trademark is not authorized by, associated with or sponsored by the trademark owner.

ACKNOWLEDGMENTS

First of all I would like to thank and congratulate you on purchasing this book. I would also like to thank my family and friends, who all selflessly helped me in writing this book. Special thanks to those who asked, insisted and assisted me in turning my ideas into this book form. All Rights Reserved 2012-2015 @ Megan Coulter.

Table of Contents

ACKNOWLEDGMENTS 5

INTRODUCTION 7

Chapter 1 - What Is Spirituality? 9
    What Is Spirituality? 12
    Spirituality & Stress Relief............................12
    Discovering Your Spiritual Self 19
    Nurturing Relationships 20
    Living A Spiritual Life 21
    Disconnecting From Physical World 22
    Religion & Spirituality 24
    Connection Between Spirituality And Religion 26

Chapter 2 - Spirituality & Healthcare............28
    Spirituality In Physical Health.......................30
    Spirituality In Mental Health........................31

How Far Spirituality Helped People Cope Up With Mental Health Problems?..........32

Spirituality In Parenting 35

When Spirituality Doesn't Work? 37

Chapter 3 - Why A Person Should Be Spiritual?..40

Spirituality – A Complicated Subject for Researchers...41

Health Benefits Of Being Spiritual................42

Some Helpful Tips 49

Using Spirituality To Relieve Stress..............51

Chapter 4 - Spiritual Therapy........................55

What Is Spiritual Healing?............................58

Other Forms of Healing................................60

How Can Spiritual Healers Help You? 64

Verdict..68

Chapter 5 - Understanding Spiritual Healing 70

What Needs Healing and Why? 71

Spiritual Healing Techniques 73
Spiritual Healing in Treating Cancer 77
The Essence Of Spiritual Healing Prayer 81
Spiritual Healing Energies & Their Secrets ... 84

Chapter 6 - Spirituality In Grief 108
Some Common Things You Shouldn't Say to a Grieving Person 113
Managing Grief Through Grief Counseling 122

Chapter 7 - How Spirituality Helps Recover From Addiction 128
How Spirituality Cures Addiction & Substance Abuse? 129
Benefits of Spiritual Recovery Programs 135
How Religion Keeps Teen Away from Substance Abuse? 137

DISCLAIMER 139
MORE FROM AUTHOR 140
ABOUT AUTHOR 155

INTRODUCTION

The book "**Spiritual Healing – *An Innovative Approach For Compassionate, Effective Spiritual Health And Healing***" is recommended to all individuals, spiritual care providers, and students to gain the insightful knowledge about spirituality and religion. We wrote this book with our extensive research, training and real life experience in the areas of health and spirituality. Group of students, interested individuals, and professionals in the disciplines of theology, social work, occupational therapy and psychology can use this eBook for guidance.

Initially, we would introduce you with the concept of spirituality and religion and the ways to discover your inner self. Here, we will try to explore the spiritual dimension in ourselves. We will try to understand the relationship between spirituality, religion and healthcare. These days, spirituality has been witnessing wider acceptance from the individuals as well as healthcare providers.

Spirituality has received great interest in media and people started pursuing their individual spiritual growth. But there are certain aspects in our personal life where we need something more than spirituality, where spirituality doesn't work. Here, we will discuss why everyone should be spiritual and the holistic techniques of spiritual healing. To conclude, we will explore how spirituality can be helpful to recover from substance abuse and addiction.

Chapter 1 - What Is Spirituality?

One of the best parts of spiritual insight is that you can connect yourself to something you may not have imagined ever inside you. Even though you think that you are small and limited, it is not so. According to spirituality, a divine and flawless light exists within you. This light is found in everyone, whether you know them or not. You may believe that your limits are just with your physical body, your age, gender, family, race, status in life and job. But when it comes to spirituality, there is something more than all these things within you.

The word 'spirit' seems similar to 'expire' and 'inspire'. And it is true because you feel ultimate inspiration when you are full of spiritual energy. Your time expires on this world when the spiritual energy exits your physical body.

There are two major themes of spiritual journey –
- Let yourself to be full of inspiration that is also reflected into joy, love, wisdom, service and peacefulness.
- Keeping in mind that there is a predictable expiration which is waiting to set you free of the unnecessary circumstances you are likely to believe that they are very important now.

Spirituality

When it comes to understand spirituality, the study goes deeper in the heart of everyone and it spans far beyond than we think it should be. It is not limited to the physical world we are stuck in. It is spirituality which keeps you connected to the divine and amazing powerful force which exists in the universe. It doesn't matter you are seeking inner peace, worldly success or complete enlightenment; no knowledge can drive you to attainment of goals and deliver a level of living which is more effective than what spiritual knowledge gives.

If you choose the path which is full of spirituality, it can drive you to the clearer vision for life, improved stress management and better interpersonal relationships. Some of the tools for stress relief are very physical, such as healthy eating habits, exercising and interacting with friends. On the other side, a less physical way goes through spirituality.

What Is Spirituality?

Spirituality can be defined in many ways. But in the truest sense, spirituality gives context to our lives. It is not all about a specific system of belief or religious prayer. Instead, it comes from the connection with your inner self, your search for purpose of life and your personal value system.

Spirituality takes the form of prayer, religious observance, meditation or trust in higher force. Some people may find it in music, nature, art or secular community. Different people have different beliefs about spirituality.

Spirituality & Stress Relief

Religion is a predefined set of practices and beliefs shared by a community of people about their bonding with spiritual power(s). On the flip side, spirituality is the relationship between a person and a spirit (which may be a God or a Higher Power, or is just a representation of connection of human being to the metaphysical reality which is higher than oneself). If people are just following the motions of certain practices set by the group, they are likely to be just religions, not spiritual. But there are some people who believe in being spiritual, not religious. They don't follow any particular belief system of a religion. They contemplate and still feel connected to the universe.

Religious and spiritual people follow different ways to express their qualities by attending religious services, praying, meditating, viewing, visiting nature, and getting engaged in music or art or connecting with people who have same beliefs. When it comes to stress relief, spirituality can do these things to keep you feel relaxed –

- **Creates the Feel of Stillness, Quiet and Peace** – We are likely to spend too much time rushing from different activities and trying to do different things. We also spend lots of time to distract ourselves from a lot of thoughts vigorously which are striking our minds throughout the day. By practicing spirituality, you can get quiet along with rushing around. This way, if you spend your time while praying, meditating or just accepting everything within you and around you in that present moment, you can get the space to detach yourself from the external chaos and find the ways to improve your sense of calm and gain more positive beliefs.

- **Helps You Lose Yourself** – If you believe that there is something in the world greater than you, it is possible that you realize that you are not completely responsible for every event happens in your life. Though it's not your fault, both good and bad things will happen in your life in their own, no matter what. Spirituality will let you to reduce or release the burden to blame yourself for all the bad things happen in your life and consistently forcing yourself to attain good results.

- **Increase Sense of Self** – When any unforeseen negative or positive events occur, spiritual practice is helpful to find a way to consider these events in sensible way. Here, you will ask "How to Grow Stronger?" or "What I need to Learn?" instead "Why Me?" when something unacceptable happens. These questions can heal you from negative aftereffects and fuel you up in a creative way. When good things happen, try to feel grateful.

- **Maintains the Feel of Purpose of Life** – Most of the people spend their time brainstorming what they are doing here and what's the purpose of their life. People who start believing that their life is just about unwanted tasks, meetings and "rat race" they soon start feeling stressed and depressed. But spiritual practices enhance the feeling of connectedness and purpose. It helps them look beyond these things and enhance their sense of responsibility for universe and wider community.

- **Improved Sense of Connectedness** – If you start feeling something higher than yourself, you will feel less alone and isolated. Even better, most people who come from spiritual or religious groups get various benefits of social support, such as group activities, interpersonal support, financial help, mentoring, transportation, food etc. whenever they need. In fact, most of the problems look small and simple to sort out if you understand that you are connected to the group (the universe, or higher power) which can provide solace, acceptance, strength and even solutions.

- **Higher Perspective** – With the help of spiritual practice, you can deal with various obstacles which look insoluble. This way, you can clarify your values and focus on your important goals instead of being consumed by materialistic world and some unnecessary circumstances.

When it comes to cultivate your spirituality, there are different ways. You may join a specific religious group with common beliefs to plan out your spiritual practice. It is, by far, the most formal and mainstream way. But it is not important to join a group in order to grow up in your spiritual life. Some people belong to their particular religious group but not gain any benefit from their group. Here are some other ways to nurture your spiritual self –

- Practicing meditation, prayer and relaxation techniques on daily basis.
- Keeping a notepad to write down your feelings and thoughts and have a record of your growth
- Looking for a friend or a trusted advisor, reading essays or inspirational success stories to know how to live a happy and spiritual life
- Trying to find good things in yourself and other people
- Being ready to enjoy new experiences. If you are not happy with a specific organized religion, you may try other ones. If a specific art or practice doesn't improve your spiritual self, you can try something different.
- Share your spiritual experiences with others and ask them to share their own. In such discussions, keep in

mind that various people have various spiritual beliefs and paths. So, try and avoid any temptation to see that only your path is correct and best.

Discovering Your Spiritual Self

You may have to discover yourself to uncover your spiritual self. This way you have to ask some questions to

yourself to find out what values and experiences you have –
- What makes you happy?
- What kind of relationships important for you?
- What achievements make you pride?
- What is your source of inspiration?
- Who gives you the feel of community?
- What is most valuable in your life?

By answering these questions, you can easily identify the most valuable experiences and people in your life. This information can help you focus on relationships, and the activities that are most important for you. These answers can describe you as person.

Nurturing Relationships

Spirituality also helps nurture your relationships with your loved ones and friends. In essence, it is important to foster your relationships with the important people. It can enhance a deep sense of your purpose in life. You can prioritize relationships with family and friends. Give them more than you get. Volunteer to your community and accept people as they are, without any judgment. Try to see the good things in yourself and people.

Living A Spiritual Life

Stay connected to your inner self and the lifestyle of the people around you. It can improve your physical and mental quality of life. With real life experiences and age, your individual point of view about spirituality may change. But it can help you cope up with stress, whether small or large. It makes the sense of well-being and defines the purpose of your life.

Disconnecting From Physical World

Probably, the ideal way to get connected with the spiritual self is to detach with the most physical and materialistic world.

- **Spiritual Approach** – It is the way to look something more than the external appearances and all the 5 senses to your intuitive viewpoint to find out the causes related to your outer conditions. With the help of spiritual approach, someone can change and uplift their environment by improving and transforming their own vision.

- **Materialistic Approach** – It completely relies on experiential evidences from all the 5 senses – that can be heard, seen, touched, tasted and smelled. The outcomes of this approach rely on how external things appear and to decide what and how to feel and think of them. With the help of materialistic approach, a person can fix anything wrong or displaced in their outer world by making changes and moving things.

Spirituality is basically about looking within and understanding what you look within yourself. The outer world is temporary, ephemeral, and ever changing. Our physical body will be dead someday, leaving all such worldly accessories away. On the flip side, your inner realm is eternal, timeless and intensely reflective.

Religion & Spirituality

Even though spirituality and religion are used with each other sometimes, they actually define two unique parts of experiences. Spirituality is often seen as the supernatural part of religion.

Spirituality

But spirituality is a source of divinity which flows and pulsates as the essence and wellspring of soul. It relates to your inner search to find the greater purpose and sense of your existence. Here are some of the important elements of spirituality –

- Respect and love for good
- Respecting and loving yourself
- Respecting and loving everyone
- Looking ahead of external appearances and the deeper soul and significance of everything

Religion basically describes a culture or an organized group which is mostly being influenced by the divine or spiritual soul. Usually, religion acts with an intention and mission to provide particular doctrines and teachings while spreading and developing a specific way of life.

Connection Between Spirituality And Religion

Different religions have different rituals and beliefs. Some followers bend over vivid idols of deities, while some listen to inspired lectures and dressed in Sunday robes. And some followers pray 5 times a day by bending over to touch their heads to the ground. Irrespective of various techniques of worship, the purpose of all religions is spirituality. And all the religions have the essence of the Supreme Thing or God.

In short, spirituality contains all religions but it is beyond all religions. Or it contains all the sciences and philosophies but it is beyond them. Respecting and loving all the images of God and religions doesn't really mean you need to agree with and follow all their rituals. It is not even necessary to agree with and believe all the doctrines and elements in the religion you follow. Just do whatever is right for you and others.

Spirituality

Let yourself to be full of inspiration, which can be related to joy, wisdom, service or peacefulness.

Chapter 2 - Spirituality & Healthcare

For most of the people, religion and spirituality have been proved very valuable and helpful for the people. We interviewed to people with various religions like Muslim, Christianity, Sikhism, Jewish and Buddhism and those who don't believe in following a particular religion. Spirituality has different meanings for different people. But there are many people who have trust in the existence of Allah or God. In fact, some people said that they didn't get any benefit with all that.

Is it possible to enjoy healthier lifestyle with family with spirituality? According to recent medical studies, spiritual people are less likely to have self-damaging behaviors like smoking, suicide, alcohol and drug abuse, and they have complete life satisfaction and less stress in their lives.

In most of the researches, physical and spiritual sense is found only in elderly people. But we have also found a glimpse of possibility in having good health and spiritual well-being in people of all age groups. Though spirituality has been proved to improve blood circulation, reduce depression and improve immunity, it is better if religious beliefs don't interfere with medical help. So, how spirituality can improve your family's health? And what spirituality exactly is?

Megan Coulter

Spirituality In Physical Health

When it comes to medical science, scientists and doctors once overlooked the results of spirituality. According to most recent findings, the faith and religion are helpful to fight disease and promote good health by providing extra social support like religious groups and improving ability to cope up with health condition with prayer and a belief of having a purpose in all things. However, research has not been done on kids. But several studies found out positive outcomes on adults with spirituality.

A study conducted for 7 years on elderly people. In this study, religious involvement led to less depression and less physical disability. With the major religious holidays, the death rates were also lowered than expected. In those cases, faith was found to postpone death rates.

Here, elderly people who participated in religious services regularly had stronger immunity than those who didn't involve in all these activities. These people also had higher chances of controlled blood pressure. Patients having open-heart operation who had religious ties got comfort and strength from their religion found with much higher chances to survive than those who didn't believe in religion.

Spirituality In Mental Health

Spiritual and religious beliefs are found to be very important for dealing with hardships and tough times. Faith is the source of purpose and guidelines. If you are having a tough time with health problems, your religious practices and beliefs can help you deal with the feelings of helplessness, manage life situations, restore meaning of life and help you regain the feeling of control. Spirituality is found powerful and valuable source of potency for many families.

Even medical studies accepted and confirmed that your mental well-being can be improved with spirituality. A study was conducted on men who were undergoing medical help. Religion was proved helpful to cope up with illness. In another study, people with high levels of optimism and hope helped them fight depression because they strictly followed their religion.

How Far Spirituality Helped People Cope Up With Mental Health Problems?

We talked to most people who felt that spirituality helped them very much in dealing with mental health issues. Regular visits to their religious groups and prayers helped them very much, even in hospital. For some people, independent meditation was found helpful. Even those who didn't have faith in God or prayer, meditation sessions were proved beneficial for their mental health. According to some people, support from other members and belief in God helped them cope up with suicidal tendencies.

Religion and spirituality also helped people to survive in depression and grief, probably with a faith that 'they are not alone'. A woman confirmed that she would be depressed if she didn't hear about spirituality. The concept of forgiving and loving God, for whom everyone is equal, provided comfort to many people. Some people felt that they got inspiration, courage, patience and strength from spirituality. Their faith helped them survive in various mental conditions.

However, there are many people who believe that religion is not the only thing that makes you feel fulfilled. There is a limit in how far it helps you to overcome depression and other devastating conditions. According to them, prayer is helpful only if they use it with proper medical help or medication.

While some people revealed that they survived through the problems and improved their conditions through spirituality. Many people stopped smoking and drinking alcohol when they started doing prayer. Some people diagnosed with schizophrenia stopped having drugs and alcohol when they started going to church and their sleeping patterns were improved with prayer. After getting healing charm and visiting Mecca, many people with grief started having healthy meals again and felt less depressed.

Hence, religion found helpful and spirituality worked as "surviving mechanism" with therapeutic benefits of relaxation, rebalancing and distraction. It gave some people a purpose to move on. Prayer acts as the path to "bottling things up". Meditation is considered something that one can do at anywhere, anytime.

Spirituality In Parenting

Attending religious services and organized events are helpful for some families to strengthen their spiritual values. But religion is not the only solution. Parents and children can find spiritual sense in some less traditional paths.

To promote the sense of spirituality in your family, you have to consider your own values. Consider what's more important to you? How well do your everyday activities show your values? Do you avoid things that matter the most because you are busy in doing things that are less important?

Here Are Other Tips To Foster Spirituality In Your Family –

- **Examine Your Roots** – While exploring the past you shared, both you and your children connect with the values of past and gain more sense of the values and history of your family.

- **Consider How Much You're Involved in Community** – If you are involved in a community, you may never like to play a larger role. If you never participated in a community, first investigate them around you.

- **Remember How you Felt at Birth of Your Child** – Get back to the past in your mind and recall the dreams and hopes you had.

- **Share Some Silent Moments with Children** – Take a meditation for a few minutes with them or alone. Think of your life as a person, and your parenthood. And spend some time with kids discussing such thoughts with kids and let them give you some ideas about spirituality.

- A nature walk can become your spiritual guide and a source of information. It can give you relaxation and you can explore the wonders around you.

- Read some books with kids which have spiritual ideas and share your ideas of what you are learning.

You may conduct this search on your own or with a larger community, friends or your family. Start a journey of spirituality to live a healthier life for you and your family.

When Spirituality Doesn't Work?

Some people told that religion or spirituality doesn't work sometimes.

According to the state of mind of a person, it can make things worse. Some people found religion and their practices helpful when everything was going well. It didn't help when one felt unwell. Some people with psychotic depression explained how they got helped to overcome their negative thoughts and control them with Buddhism. According to them, meditation was helpful to deal with psychotic episodes. But when the conditions were worse, it was nearly impossible to meditate. Hence, prayer was not found helpful.

Religion helped people to deal with mental health conditions, suicidal thoughts and weird feelings. But some people described that their spiritual sense was nothing when they felt unwell. In severe cases, only medical help works. Some people were found offended by religious leaders and religions. According to them, people are prone to learn some unquestioning and misguided belief. These groups taught them to discriminate against those with mental health issues rather than accepting them. This way, some created their own spirituality and some lost their faith on it

    As a result, most people considered themselves as spiritual, not religious. They have greater feeling, some intuition, but they feel hesitant to joining institutions. In reality, there are some institutions which are based on making a sensible change and tie a group together. Institutions can be dictatorial, slow or plodding. And they can even shield and help wrongdoings. But institutions are the only way to perpetuate our actions and ideas.

    Spirituality is based on emotions and religion is based on obligation. When spirituality relaxes you, your religion mobilizes you. It is religion which creates aid organizations.

Chapter 3 - Why A Person Should Be Spiritual?

Do people have any benefit with being religious or having some non-religious set of beliefs related to spirituality which help them in everyday life over others who don't have such things, when it comes to improve physical and mental health? According to a research, spirituality and religion are helpful for some people to better deal with stress, depression and illness.

Though spirituality and religion are not enough to cure any critical illness, they can, at least, have positive impact on your health. Several research studies showcased the connection between religious practices and beliefs. They are responsible for reduced risk of threatening habits like substance abuse, smoking and suicidal thoughts. Some studies proved that the life expectancy improves among people who are engaged constant religious practices. They are more likely to enjoy their life despite chronic pain and certain health issues.

Spirituality – A Complicated Subject for Researchers

Spirituality is proved to be a very complicated subject for researchers when it comes to frame its concepts in scientific terms. One main reason is that spirituality cannot be explained in a particular definition. Spirituality is strictly associated with religious beliefs of some people. And some are those who associate it with art, meditation, nature or inner harmony and peace. Some researchers believe that determining spirituality with points related to harmony, peacefulness and well-being doesn't make sense. It is because spirituality is just described as improved mental condition. So, spirituality is defined in terms of religious beliefs and practices.

According to a researcher, "Spirituality is a multidimensional, valuable part of human experience which is really hard to measure or understand completely with any scientific method. There is no solid evidence in medical science which proves its therapeutic benefit in medical conditions. Spirituality is defined by the Association of American Medical Colleges and is documented as factor that affects health of different people. The spirituality is a concept found in all societies and cultures. It can be expressed in the search of a person for ultimate sense of solace by participating in any religious practice or having faith in family, God, rationalism, naturalism, arts and humanism.

Health Benefits Of Being Spiritual

Despite what the medical researches and studies claim, it is undeniably true that there is no replacement of the feeling of believing in yourself. Spirituality is the path to find the meaning and purpose of life. We have done our own research and found that having faith in higher force and religion have their own perks. It is proved that religious practice is all about better physical, social and mental health. Have a look at the benefits of being spiritual.

Increases Lifespan

Most people don't expect to live more than 84th birthday in the world if everything goes well, when it comes to physical and mental health. But religion can help people add a few more years to their lives, according to a research. According to a review published in 2011 edition of Explore magazine, people who have strong spiritual and religious belief enjoyed around 18% higher life expectancy.

It shows the addition of around 7 years of age to their lifespan on average. The reason is simple. Religion is likely to dishearten self-destructive habits like drinking, smoking and drug abuse. The believers in religion and spirituality are more likely to have better eating habits and they do exercise more. As a result, these factors have been proved more helpful to improve their hormonal, cardiovascular, brain and immune health. According to a research on 7th Day Adventists, religion helped men to live around 8.9 years longer than average age and women to live around 3.6 years longer than average who have higher risks of heart disease and cancer. With participating in religious and spiritual practices, the risk was reduced to 66%.

Reduces Stress Levels

Have you ever noticed how people who have faith in a higher power are more likely to deal with emotional storms than others who don't practice such things? The reality is that religion is related to greater mental health. In the Journal of Religion & Health, a study was published which reported that women engaged in religious practices have 27% lesser risks of depression and are 57% more likely to lead healthier life than those who are not doing all these things.

According to Lisa Johnson, a psychologist, spiritual people are less likely to lead stressful life due to several reasons. However, the argument about the connection between religion and mental health is going on psychological basis. In the research, some of the processes that are helpful and recommended include gratitude, mindfulness, altruism, empathy, higher social support and improved sense of connectedness. According to researches and their viewpoint on the subject, religion and spirituality help people deal with sickness, loss and trauma. It is because religion gives them purpose of life and meaning to such events. They can get practical tools to face their problems. They endure stress and become stronger by joining the community of helpful people. After all, *a problem solved is problem halved.*

Inspires You to Thrive

Self-discipline and confidence are the attributes and common qualities of religious people and they develop over time. Religious beliefs motivate people to be reliable, loyal, self-disciplined, hard working, and altruistic, according to Dr. Koenig who says that these qualities are also helpful in professional life. All these attributes help improve business and social relationships in long term.

The belief in a higher power, or spirituality, is likely to provide a long-term source of reliable comfort and the sense of personal worth and value. It also enhances the confidence to take healthy risks and explore the world. Sometimes, suicidal thoughts and depression often go untreated and unnoticed and they get severe. If you are suffering from these problems and don't want them to affect your life anymore, spirituality is the way to completely free yourself of these life hazards.

Improves Relationships

If you invite a third person into your personal life, you may probably be risking your relationship. It is sort of something we would not recommend. Instead, you can add spiritual content to your life and improve your bonds with your loved one. Spirituality is the way that healed the life of many couples over the centuries. When you get to believe that a trusted higher power is doing something good in your life, you are likely to bring all the love and feeling of compassion to your relationship.

As an added bonus, it forms the intense pleasure of connectedness. A study was conducted on the Italian-American community which was closely knit in Pennsylvania. It was found that the death rate was shorted down to half than the national average from heart attack. Strong social bonding was one of the helpful factors. You can easily connect with others in spiritual communities and share your friendship and love with others. It helps improve your health, immunity and overall wellbeing greatly.

Makes You Feel Grateful

When it comes to spending the whole day at work and traveling from home to work and vice versa, it is really challenging to make time to remember all the things you feel lucky to have. But once you make habit to do so, it can give you a welcoming boost to your overall wellbeing. In the Journal of Personality & Social Psychology, the series of studies was published where it shows that practicing gratitude daily and listing out all the things you are grateful for can add brighter outlook to your lifestyle and add a higher sense of positivity.

Spirituality

But there is no role of spirituality here. Though spirituality and gratitude are not related to each other, some studies have proved that spirituality can improve your ability to feel grateful. If you start doing religious practices and activities, you will be more likely to have higher feeling of gratitude in all aspects of your daily life. Religion improves gratefulness and religious people also feel grateful to someone in their life. As a result, it makes the person feel good. It improves brain functions and people are likely to be healthy. The more you practice spirituality, the more you feel grateful and the better life quality will be.

Some Helpful Tips

If you want to improve your spiritual health, you should try the following tips as suggested by the American Academy of Family Physicians –

- Volunteer and engage in certain community activities
- Recognize the things in life which can give you the feeling of compassion, inner peace, strength or connectedness to a higher power or others
- Make some time each day to perform activities that makes you spiritual, i.e. praying, attending religious services, doing yoga, meditation, or reading inspirational book you love or taking nature walk

According to a study, you should also practice forgiveness. If you are willing to forgive others, it can improve your mental health and you can have greater satisfaction with life, higher self-esteem, and less anxiety, depression and anger.

Using Spirituality To Relieve Stress

When there are many ways to find a Higher Power or God, study suggests that people who start their journey enjoy happier life and better health and relief from stress. There are many people who are spiritual and religious join a religious community which helps them and shows the best ways to reduce stress. Here are some research-based and proven ways to relieve stress with spirituality -

Prayer

It can help you feel more connected with god and leave you with safer, calmer and more grounded feel which can work as shock absorber against all your stresses. You can also feel the benefits which are quite similar to that of meditation, such as higher immunity, lower blood pressure and improved heart health.

Show Your Gratitude

Even though the benefits of showing gratitude to god are common among elder people, it has been connected with improved health conditions. Showing gratitude can also reduce the feeling of stress and help you deal with depression. You can keep a notepad handy in which you can list down all the things you have and you feel grateful for. It is one effective way to improve your gratitude. So, whenever you feel low next time, see this list to pick yourself up and notice all the good things in life and write them down.

Be Intrinsically Oriented

Just like having many faiths, there are several ways to experience the religion with a faith. Some people express their spiritual self inherently, in a more personal approach. They dedicate their life to become a good person or to devote themselves to god. Some use their religious part to fulfill external needs like improving their standing in the community and finding friends. As per a research, you can enjoy greater benefits if you are more intrinsically oriented.

Follow Optimism

If you are having a tough time, keep in mind a phrase, "When a door is closed, God opens a Window." People who trust good more than anything else in this world, they are likely to be more optimistic. There are various options for you to have trust on your God and develop more inner control. Have trust on your abilities, your situations, and your God.

Find Valuable Lessons to Learn from Tough Situations

Spiritual people are more likely to see stressful situations as the way to grow strong and even learn a valuable lesson from a higher power. It is the best way to view any stressful situation as a challenge to you. This feeling can make the tough situations less devastating. The less threatened you feel, the more you are physically ready to deal with stress. You are more likely to find best ways to cope up with difficulties and even turn tough situation into a way to greater personal growth and better life quality.

Using Law of Attraction

Law of Attraction is something which has been practiced for centuries. People are discussing a lot about its principle over the web. According to this law, whatever you think of is what you attract. It means if you are constantly feeling bad about your life, you are attracting bad events in life. If you focus on anything you want to happen in life, you will attract more positive things.

Chapter 4 - Spiritual Therapy

Spiritual Therapy is a unique way of freeing your mind of irrational thoughts and energies and restoring positive energy in both body and mind. It is also about analyzing your spiritual and emotional consciousness in a natural way. It includes every aspect, from physical to mental healing and also known as **Holistic Therapy**.

Individuals suffering from emotional imbalances and mental depression can easily rely on certain kinds of spiritual therapy in order to overcome their obstacles. It is a kind of metaphysical healing which is about recognizing your own healing powers. The person may put their beliefs in a higher power for help or just draw beliefs and strengths from inside in this kind of therapy. It helps to gain self-confidence and feel energized. This therapy is capable to deal with different forms of distress like relationship issues, grief and daily stress.

You can seek spiritual guidance from special seminars. You may talk to a spiritual therapist. Spiritual therapists try to know about your personal situation by working closely with you. Then he will assess all the situations to determine your weakness and how you will be benefitted with this therapy. These sessions are possible over phone in some cases if you feel uncomfortable or cannot be there in person.

Some kinds of sessions cover deeper meditation. It is performed in order to attain the higher level of enlightenment. Some forms of meditations are performed in classroom or group setting. Some forms are done on one-on-one personal sessions. Some forms of therapy also provide hypnosis as the important part of healing or treatment.

Despite having some exceptions, spiritual therapy is usually based on healing from moral or religious concept. Some forms of spiritual therapy are based on religion. Some of them include Jewish spiritual healing or Christian spiritual healing therapy. It also includes New Age therapy.

There is a new and unique approach employed by SRT or Spiritual Response Therapy. This method is often be performed by incorporating a psychic. It is supposed to be helpful to deal with harsh memories from the past and subconscious thoughts which are causing trouble in healing process. The person engages into their subconscious mind in order to keep negative thoughts at bay and redeem peace of mind in this therapy.

What Is Spiritual Healing?

In "New Age" Movement or "Mind Body Spirit" therapy, spiritual healing plays an important role and today, it is learnt and taught. In 1976, it was considered a very controversial thing. Also in some spiritual healing groups, healing was considered as the gift for a few, instead of giving it to all.

Spiritual healing is now used to treat all kinds of conditions but some people are more accessible to this treatment than others because of several factors like mental outlook and karma. The results from healing may vary. If a patient believes in technique and have great faith on it and the healer, it will surely help the healing process. But it is not like faith healing which is practiced in most religions. Instead, it is completely based on spiritual energy. So, it is not necessary that one should have complete faith on it. Even if you are skeptical, you can still get benefits of healing from it.

Spiritual healing is helpful for the people in several ways. It sometimes, helps in various unexpected ways. Healing may, or may not, cure someone completely. It may, at least, help the patients to deal with the problem they have and they eventually become more positive. It is very rare when someone gets healing and has no improvements later on. In fact, many people found improvement and great deal of positivity in their spiritual life. And their conditions were improved where other treatments didn't work. Though miraculous things are rare, but it helps people to be open to positivity.

When we start benefitting others, we get more spiritual healing and we are likely to develop more spirituality and we become better healers than before when we develop spirituality.

Other Forms of Healing....

Faith Healing

More often than not, faith healing is something that is always being on the news. With this method, it might show the failure or success of a person to self heal with this method. Over the last couple of decades, faith healing was considered to be a controversial topic. It is nothing new that people are getting healed through faith. Some forms of healing through faith have been practiced in different religions for hundreds of years. However, various movements took shape in 19th and 20th centuries. The Peculiar People and the Emmanuel movement are some of the popular examples.

Phineas Quimby (1802-1866) was a well-known person who discovered the combination of hypnotism and magnetism in order to developed a kind of "Natural healing" therapy. He was also the mentor of Mary Baker Eddy, the founder of first leading faith healing movement. They were the Christian Scientists.

With faith healing, another group is more recent. A well-known Pentecostal preacher, Kenneth E. Hagin (1917-2003) was behind the scenes to work on it. He was responsible to develop more modern technique of healing with faith.

What is Faith Healing?
The term, "Healing through Faith" is the synonymous with any cure which is not based on medical science. It can be supernatural or psychic. Spiritual therapy is also the part of faith healing. Generally, this kind of self healing on faith is based on supernatural force. It is also known as divine healing.

What Faith Healing is all about?

While using this method, a believer is allowed to practice different approaches. They may consider practical or hands-on healing, distant healing or other methods. This method can allow anyone who may be an intended person or not. Here, the believer has to accept that some divine power is working for them and they can just believe in the power of forgiveness.

Otherwise, the person may also draw the divine inside. It can be possible through rituals, prayers or even meditation. Some people may visit the religious places like shrine or any pilgrimage or sacred place like Tibetan Monk, a Holy Man or the Lourdes in France.

If a person devotes their self on meditation instead, they seek inner healing and the process covers believing the power within to heal. It may demand the release of "Chi" energy of the body.

Once liberated, this self-healing energy helps in healing of the body during meditation.

There is no medical or scientific research which shows the declarations for healing on the basis of faith. Meditation is the only exception here. On meditation, the positive impacts have clearly been indicated by scientific research. Though the process of healing therapy may be doubtful, the effects of meditation seem to be scientifically proven.

Absent Healing

Basically, absent healing is about sending spiritual healing by praying for someone else to feel better with their Karmic pattern. It also covers the chanting of mantra. It basically involves visualizing the person with good health condition while doing prayer. This technique improves the healing process.

Contact Healing

This approach is practiced mostly in the Aetherius Society. This technique is known as "the King Technique" by this society. It is very straightforward approach. It consists of cleansing the aura of the patient and sending the spiritual energy into the area of discomfort and some of the main chakras through physical contact and visualization. The session usually takes half an hour.

How Can Spiritual Healers Help You?

Are you looking for spiritual healers? Are you wondering how they are going to help you? Do you want to gain some spiritual knowledge by solving questions in your mind?

Spirituality is a journey to connect you to your real nature and create a harmony between your body, mind and soul. You can start the journey of exploration on your own and seek help of experts who can guide you in several spiritual quests. These experts are called as "Spiritual Healers" because they are fully aware of the reality and know how to use it to benefit others.

A Spiritual Healer Can Assist You In Following Conditions –

- If you have lost the interest of life and are feeling depressed in your life
- Overwhelmed by emotions and fears
- If you are stressed out on performing in your personal and professional life
- If you are suffering from illnesses on daily basis
- If you are unable to find the right way and are pessimistic
- If you are doing some unfulfilling things or engaged in unsatisfied relationships

A spiritual healer can help you in some of the above problems. Some healers believe that the power of healing lies within you. All you have to see its purpose and get connected with your own self. And it can be done by practicing spirituality every day.

The process of spiritual healing is so smooth that you can grasp your emotional, mental and physical self and eradicate all the negative emotions in mind and let it thrive with positive state. There are different emotions responsible to release negative energy, such as anger, anxiety and fear. Spirituality helps improve the feeling of equanimity, resiliency and relieves you from different psychological problems.

How Spiritual Healers Work?

A spiritual healer has to hold a view of stimulated awareness. It helps tune up your healing energy. They scan specific areas or whole body, such as your chest, forehead and hands with their mind. It can be possible with identifying the areas where energy is stuck or low and they consider the issues inscribed in your mind and body. It usually takes around 1 hour to complete the healing process and end the session. The number of session and duration usually depends upon the needs of your mind and body.

Different spiritual healers are known to follow different principles, such as focusing on chakras, aura healing, visualization and past life therapy.

Can They Teach Us Spirituality?

One of the most important responsibilities of a spiritual healer is to share what they know about spirituality and use the same to guide others. The Spiritual Healers play two-fold roles in it. They heal people with their expertise and impart their guidance and knowledge in a way that others can heal on their own. They are also called as energy healers because they heal people with positive energy.

They use their thought power in an influential way in order to help sufferers to deal with their mental and psychological illnesses. There are different ways these healers can help you. They are also teaching the mantras and prayers according to your needs. You can recite them daily to improve self-awareness and positive energy within you.

They can introduce you to several spiritual mediums like meditation or energy healing, along with some breathing exercises. Meditation is considered to be one of the effective ways to enlighten your mind and attain spirituality. Meditation is the process practiced for centuries to help individuals explore their spiritual self and come out with the energy which can help improve the healing process.

Verdict

Spiritual healing is not an alternative therapy. Instead, it is just a complementary therapy. Hence, you can use it along with proper medical help. Don't use it as an alternative to medications. It is important for spiritual healers to suggest their patients not to avoid medications and professional help. Spiritual healing is just an additional support, not a guarantee to cure.

Chapter 5 - Understanding Spiritual Healing

Spiritual healing is not as difficult to understand as it seems. The term "Spiritual Energy" refers to healing by soul, spirit or a divine energy. It is also known as "Chi" energy in Chinese Cultures. Similarly, it is "ki" in Japan and "Prana" in India. It is possible with the awareness or presence of a spiritual healer.

The practice of soul healing and searching is widespread among several cultures. People are practicing spiritual healing in North America, Europe, Africa, South America, Asia and Africa. People engaged in healing with the spirit and divine soul, have cured everyone who fell ill. They have tried spiritual practices in different ways to ensure the recovery of the person.

People were always looking on their soul in the olden days. There were religious groups and churches who maintained this practice. Healers also found the need of soul in several holistic treatment practices. They didn't impose any restriction on their services to the body. Individuals and medical professionals have started practices through healing which covered the spirit.

What Needs Healing and Why?

When it comes to observations and practices, the spirit or soul is immortal and doesn't demand healing at all. It is our mind which requires healing. A sound state of mind is found in a healthy body. The more you try to comprehend spiritual healing, the clear the concept becomes. You have to try different methods to achieve this goal of healing. You have to understand your needs, desires and preferences.

The major types of soul or spiritual healing are divided into different ways.

They are classified with their origins; say Western, European, Eastern and Eclectic. They are also categorized with methods like hands-free, hands-on and distance healing. Several spiritual healing approaches may involve the use of energy, such as

- Shiatsu
- Reiki
- Therapeutic Touch (TT)
- Healing Touch (HT)
- Acupuncture
- Acupressure

The power of healing also includes prayer. It is also done with proper harmony with meditation and Yoga or as a Buddhist practice. Self-healing is also possible with meditation practices.

On an average, demise may seem too far on daily basis but it is never too soon to determine death. We all have to accept our possible demise. We have to keep it into consideration and consider whether our mind is ready to accept this tough challenging. By believing on the spiritual part of death, it is possible to prepare ourselves for everything comes along the way while staying spiritually and physically active at present.

There is no single way everyone can choose through the healing process. There are different ways to access the healing. For some people, meditation is the solution. For some people, energy healing is the way, such as Shiatsu, Qigong and Reiki and other traditional methods. Some of the modern forms like Healing Touch also used. For some, Prayer is yet another way. Whatever approach you pick, make sure that you are confident with it.

Spiritual Healing Techniques

Spiritual healers use different techniques of spiritual healing to help people around the world to achieve spiritual peace. If you are in a state where medicines are no longer helpful, you may want to seek some divine help. If restlessness of your life or mind overpowers you, it's a time to seek spiritual assistance.

Spiritual healing is mostly confused with energy healing, which is based on the fact that our body uses energy for healing and is made of energy. Instead, **spiritual healing needs involvement of awareness and healer brings it to you**.

The Aura & Chakra System

The aura and chakra chelation is related to a great human energy field where body is inscribed and generated. There are seven major chakras and seven layers of aura. It is known to be one of the primeval healing techniques which involve balancing and cleaning the aura.

In this method, we all are covered by life energy and it is being used by our body all the time. By using the power of visualization and meditation, you can gain significant strength as life energy. You can practice it by opening yourself to the spiritual force.

Thoughtform

Thoughtform is the technique which is used over the energy field of a practitioner. It protects the work you do and to sow into the field of the healing path. It is visualization or an idea. It has a particular shape which may be a colored cloud or a more complex geometric form. It has information that can support and guide you through the healing process. It is really difficult to find out the needs of your soul and it is not easy to invent the thoughtform. It is more than healing.

Aura & Chakra Surgery

According to the level of perception, you can sense, see or understand the morphology of the field of energy, such as the chakras and the structure of field. If you try to do it, you can get proper information that can help you fix distorted or broken lines or the entire part of field.

You need to manage healing techniques with extreme caution, integrity and care. You need to keep your sense of your personality aside to interact with your best. When you touch or get close to other person, several events may occur in your energy fields, minds and bodies. While using this healing technique, your inner sense may not be able to control and recognize all the existing interactions.

Spiritual healers use several other healing techniques, such as channeling, guided imagery, affirmations, visualizations and mantras. There are various techniques of spiritual healing which stand at the core of all the above methods. According to my personal experience and observations, the power of healing varies according to how much healer is aware of, not based on any healing method or approach.

When a healer practices the technique, they actually start from putting a natural skill into practice, learning a technique or both. At a certain point of time, it is possible that you observe that **awareness is the best healer**. When it comes to awareness, it doesn't matter for a healer if they are using a Thoughtform or Aura and Chakra system.

All you have to hold the awareness at high level. Healing is possible with the presence of healing and the awareness has the sense of the identity of healer. It is something that is beyond any spiritual healing method or technique.

Spiritual Healing in Treating Cancer

The real strength of spiritual healing lies within its potential to raise mental power and improve peace of mind. According to medical professionals, cancer is among the most life-threatening and painful medical conditions. Feeling cancer as a serious medical condition is the start of your spiritual journey, which is full of various emotions and upheavals, such as pain and trauma, ups and downs, turmoil and calmness. Finally, it leads to transformation and healing.

Initially, when the person is diagnosed, he or she experiences serious adverse effect on their emotional, mental and spiritual self. The terrible nature of this condition can shake the positivity of even a strongest person. A cancer patient undergoes serious physical pain and mental conflict.

The management and treatment of cancer is also very painful. It includes chemotherapy, radiation therapy and monoclonal antibody treatment. These processes can leave you with an extreme mental trauma. With such a huge disastrous situation where death seems easier than to survive, where can one find strength? There are different techniques of spiritual healing which give the power to heal and thrive.

How Spiritual Healing Helps Cancer Patients?

Even though spirituality remains underestimated, it still plays a vital role in mental and physical healing of a person. With spirituality, one can explore their inner self. With the help of spirituality, one can combat diseases and illnesses, and gain the strength to survive through pain and trauma related to the illness and find the way to peace and wellness.

Spirituality is considered very helpful to bring the mind, body and soul together. This procedure of connecting body, mind and soul together is at the core of spiritual healing. Spiritual cancer healing is helpful for the patients to deal with stress, depression and anxiety and teaches them to attain the inner peace with mental relaxation and emotional control. With the help of spiritual healing, one can learn to control and combat various symptoms of cancer like fatigue, sickness and pain.

There are various ways to find mental, emotional and physical healing for cancer patients and here are some of the popular spiritual healing processes –

Energy Healing – Seeking help of energy healers or spiritual healers is one of the ideal ways to attain healing from cancer. It is natural and powerful process which can be possible by focusing our attention to the life force, such as Prana or Chi Energy. Energy Healing is the process which includes various breathing techniques. With the complete control of this energy, the healing process of your body starts.

Prayers – It is yet another most powerful way to attain spirituality. You can heal yourself from within. Prayer has the power to help you find strength, courage and guidance to enhance healing. Prayers are widely used to gain strength to combat mental trauma and physical pain.

Quantum touch and Meditation are yet other ways of spirituality that are helpful for cancer patients to get relaxation and spiritual healing and reduce pain.

The Essence Of Spiritual Healing Prayer

Narrating the prayer is really very easy way of self-healing which is offered in your spiritual path. Prayer is supposed to make deep impact on your soul. It provides ability and power to heal. The prayer is usually devoted to a deity or Lord and helps the healer to get blessings. You can pray at the very moment and practice it every day to enjoy long-term benefits.

Spirituality includes some techniques that have no relation with religion, particularly in Western culture. It also includes meditation. Here, the intention of prayer is likely to be different than religion. Prayer is considered to be a bonding with our basic nature. It is more than an invocation and a request. Rather than driving life as per our individual interest and need and to seek help, it is all about being a friend of the Lord.

A spiritual prayer can connect you with yourself and channelize the positive energy in your body and mind. The prayer is something that helps you in healing. Healing power usually comes with a prayer. Understanding more about the spiritual prayer is the best and only way to know this power.

The Healing Power of Spiritual Prayers

Healing prayers are subject to differ according to the situation you are going to face in your life. It is also about

Spirituality

the step you are going to take in your growth. The power of healing prayer and spiritual care lies in your ability and yourself to make relationship with the higher force. Your inner intent is the base of spiritual power. The more your intent is strong and aligned and you are sure about the way to use it, the more the powerful the prayer is. If you are doing prayer like this, you can realize and understand the real essence of spiritual healing.

The spiritual healing prayer is the source to get the power from the Supreme Being. The healing prayer gives you spiritual protection and you can get to realize your real strength and nature and you can deal with your mental or physical pain. It can heal you from within. It will be helpful if you are dealing with physical wound because of long-term illness or accident. You can go through this way to deal with various problems in life.

Spiritual prayer is a type of meditation which connects you to the Supreme Being. You can learn how to focus on spiritual self with this power and experience the same energy which has created the whole universe.

Spiritual Healing Energies & Their Secrets

You may call Energy Healing an "**Energy Therapy**" or "**Energy Medicine**". Energy healing is the developed form of alternative and complementary medicine. This concept is not modern. The history of this form of energy dates back to the ancient era. It is also noted in various Eastern and Western religions, as well as in Christianity.

Energy healing was the part of several traditional approaches. The medical practitioners were used to believe that people go ill when energy goes out of control in the body. Medical practitioners suggest correcting this energy imbalance in order to heal the body in Asian countries. For instance, Japan and China have designed a medical system which is based on energy healing.

When it comes to healing energy, the faith is not limited to the physical form. Medical practitioners based on Traditional Chinese Medicine (TCM) have also found the holistic effect in Chi energy. Simply put, the amount and quality of energy revolving inside the body affect our mental, emotional and spiritual well-being. This energy is not limited to physical health.

Energy Healing

Energy healing can be defined as part of complementary and alternative medicine. It uses various methods to manipulate and changes the flow of energy. It replenishes, realigns, and stabilizes the quality and quantity of energy in the body.

Using energy to restore mental, spiritual, and physical health is the part of complementary and alternative medicine. Several approaches are used by the practitioners in order to heal the body by rotating the energy from one person to another. It will boost or reduce the levels in the body to achieve harmony. But the ability of energy to heal is still the matter of doubt for scientific researches. However, several modern medical approaches have accepted some methods like TT and Reiki as practical source of healing power.

Cosmic Energy

Healing with Cosmic Energy is the important part of spiritual healing as it involves using the energy which is found in our cosmos. It is known as the life force which keeps the balance of the entire space.

It is also called as the energy of great intelligence and consciousness which surround us every time and everywhere. Earth Energy is just a part of cosmic energy. You may receive cosmic energy in two ways. This energy is received while sleeping but it is not enough to keep the balance or order in our life.

Practicing spirituality is another way of getting cosmic energy. The cosmic energy we get through spirituality is more powerful and can help you heal. It also leads a happier and healthier life and drives the transformation and expansion of your consciousness.

How To Receive Cosmic Energy?

You need to learn energy healing and chakra breathing exercises to receive cosmic energy. Meditation is the simple and best way to gather this energy. Meditation makes your mind more focused to get it and cosmic energy usually enters through your mind. It enters our mind-body system through chakras and supports the field of human energy. Chakras are partially closed in most humans most of the time due to the distractions like fear, worry, anxiety, negative emotions and stress in mind.

The mind and body are likely to unite when you meditate. It is the best way to get the energy in your spiritual and physical self and it is also helpful in healing. Experts also suggest breathing meditation to channelize the cosmic energy in your body. You can make your mind calm with breathing meditation and it helps develop inner peace. You can practice breathing meditation in a quiet place on regular basis. You can get cosmic energy whenever your mind is calm.

In order to instantly increase energy in your body, you have to focus on breathing and absorb energy through base chakra. You can get grounding from earth energy healing and it is the good exercise to provide support to your body. Reiki is also a great method to get the cosmic energy and it works on accessing internal energy and cosmic energy.

How Far Cosmic Energy is Helpful?

When you get this energy from your inner self or through a healer, you can heal through cosmic energy. The positive energy is always helpful to heal your physical, mental and spiritual self. Cosmic energy is helpful to heal you from within. The body and mind are adorned in the energy field which is truly nourished by this energy. With our activity, we produce both negative and positive energies. We face several health problems when we release negative energy. With the help of cosmic energy, you can remove or reduce the negative energy and make peace. Here are some of its physical benefits –

- It reduces pressure on heart and improves blood flow in the body
- It lowers cortisol and lactate levels which are related to stress
- It helps reduce free radicals

- It removes all the physical problems, such as anxiety, depression and irratibility
- It forms higher skin resistance and heals heart disease
- It sharpens memory
- It improves your psychological health with promoting the feelings of rejuvenation and self-actualization

To experience all the benefits of healing with cosmic energy, you have to follow some spiritual paths and practice meditation that can open the door to receive this life force. It is better if you contact the healer.

Earth Energy

Healing with Earth Healing is the technique of self healing with which, the person uses the energy from earth and improves positive energy to heal oneself and enjoy more fulfilled life. Earth energy is known to be the vital force which one can receive from earth directly. You may also receive earth energy from any living object which is rooted to earth, such as animals and trees.

Here, you need to understand that your connection is deeply rooted to the earth and you can get support from earth in different ways. Earth is among those five elements with which a human body is created. The earth energy is a vital force to connect us to the universe. So, it is an important part of self healing.

How Earth Energy Works?

Healing from Earth Energy is possible only when you get energy from earth. The earth energy will flow through the human energy field, energy channels and chakras in your body. You will feel the sense of well-being and balance when earth energy circulates through the body.

Most individuals can't even realize that the poor health, diseases and lack of wellbeing can take a toll on the body when energy is less or blocked. Anxiety and stress are the psychological issues which come into existence when the positive energy goes imbalanced in the body. The feeling of ineffectiveness and depression are the results of lack of earth energy in the body.

Cosmic energy and earth energy are the most important part of positive energy in human body. Earth energy reinstates the flow of energy through the body system and heals you. It includes the rich and dense vibration so you can feel connected to your physical body.

How to Receive Earth Energy?
There are different steps you may follow in your daily life to become the recipient of earth energy. Here are some of the popular and easy ways to receive earth energy –

- Stand on the ground or grass bare feet to touch the earth energy with your feet. There are higher chances of

Spirituality

receiving earth energy when you are barefoot.
- Greet the earth with compassion, love and gratitude
- Once earth energy reaches seventh chakra, you can feel the energy in your aura
- You can feel the earth energy traveling through your feet and moving up your knees. It can improve healing when it moves from feet to the knees.

In order to receive earth energy, you can try silent praying or meditation to focus on relieving pain and stress you are facing. Release the negative energy which is the root cause of your stress or pain on the earth. You have to focus your mind on it.

The major benefit of Earth Energy healing is that you can deal with all the common illnesses in your daily life and relieve yourself from joint pain. It also improves air and blood circulation in your body and you can easily heal high blood pressure and other medical conditions. Earth Energy comprises of subtle and natural form of electrical energy which also helps in reversing aging process.

Transformational Energy

Healing with Transformational Energy is often considered as expanding the benefits of energy healing. In reality, it is based on transforming the health or consciousness by combining various energy healing techniques. It facilitates the transformation at consciousness. We are covered by transformational and positive energies which can heal our body. It is known by different names in different countries, such as Prana in India, Chi in China etc.

This energy is also known as life energy. This energy can flow from one object to other and from one person to another to influence them.

How It Works?

Transformational energy is helpful in clearing and cleansing the consciousness of an individual on spiritual, mental and physical level. At the certain point of time, we experience stress, trauma and pain and infections and diseases. These are the causes of the flow of negative energy in the body. One thing you should keep in mind is that you should draw and accept the positive energy from the cosmos to release the negative energy which is trapped within you.

You can acquire various kinds of spiritual energy from universal energy field in order to improve the process of healing. We can transmit and receive spiritual, psychic, and physical energy. With various spiritual processes and meditation, we can attune ourselves to the universal energy's frequency and feel the psychic and spiritual healing. The transformational energy doesn't just reduce suffering and pain, but it also cleanses your body from within. The raw power creates the state of wellbeing and sets your mind free of all the distraction and physical body from all the diseases.

How to Receive this Energy?

The best thing with transformational energy is that you can harness it. In fact, anyone can do it. You have to be at peace to hold this energy. There are different techniques or ways to control, receive and use this energy for your health. Prayers, meditation and yoga are the widely-used ways. With these techniques, you can learn to focus your mind on one object or area. You have to focus on energy and have faith in it. You will feel the energy flowing into your body.

Magnetic Energy

Magnetic energy healing or aura healing is helpful to clear and realign the magnetic energy field so you can experience mental peace and good physical health. We have magnetic energy system in our body. Let's find out what is magnetic energy system to understand magnetic energy healing.

Our body has chakras which are also called as "Anchored Energy Vortexes". Our body has emotional or mental etheric and the soul. They all are connected by channels which meet into the energy vortex. Each energy center differs from another in size. Our body has hundreds of these energy centers. There is an energy field in our etheric body which covers our physical body. The central energy channel generates the energy field and runs from spine's base to forehead. All of the seven energy vortexes are connected in this central energy channel. So, whenever the energy flows through the chakras and channel in the body, an electromagnetic field is created to cover our physical body.

That electromagnetic field is at the core of healing through magnetic energy.

If any blockage occurs in the flow of energy from the vortex or the channels, it causes imbalance in the etheric body. Normally, this blockage affects the emotional, physical and mental state. This blockage is one of the major causes of anxiety, stress, depression, anger, cold or flu, joint pain and lots more.

You may feel the blockages and obstacles through warm or cold spots and the hike of tingling session. Some of the other signs of blockages in magnetic energy are light headedness, Goosebumps, numbness in a specific body part, etc. These blockages may cause nausea, serious headaches, pain in stomach or heart, diarrhea, tiredness and extreme sensitivity issues. In that case, you can work on magnetic energy and consult the spiritual healer to clear the blockage. This process of channelizing the flow and clearing the blockage is called as "Magnetic Energy Healing".

Here are some of the common benefits of healing through magnetic energy –

- It reduces stress
- It improves clarity of mind and removes doubts and confusion
- It removes all the negative and toxic thoughts to remove negative energy. It removes some of the toxic emotions, such as resentment, anger and betrayal.
- It restores the focus on career, life goals, and other things that matter most in your life
- It removes various kinds of distractions
- It strengthens your mind, body and spirit
- It deals with all types of negative energies which hamper the proper functioning of body
- It controls emotional imbalances like eating disorder, addiction and low self esteem
- It controls and removes psychological imbalances like poor

communication, feeling of insecurity and indecisiveness.
- It restores peace of mind and harmony by balancing the flow of energy through vortex and energy channel.

Vibrational Energy

Vibrational Energy can help you in mental, spiritual and emotional transformation. Vibrational Energy healing addresses the most subtle energy field level and inquires the vibrations making physical body. It is an integral energy which takes place in all of us. We perceive the materialistic world through our five senses. But we cannot perceive the energy fields with these senses. Our perceptual channels are also the form of energy. We have to broaden our awareness to perceive the energy. And it can be achieved through healers or meditation.

We have to be more adjusted to the higher perception frequencies and the energy field outside and within the body to channelize and find the vibrational energy. You can develop bio-energetic ability of some kind when you learn sensing the energy fields.

If you want to understand vibrational energy, you have to first understand its roots. Our human body is created with thousands of atoms which create molecules and form cells. These cells are helpful to form the bones, tissues, organs and muscles. But how are atoms made of?

Atoms are actually made with the subtle particles of energy or light, which are the tiniest form of vibrational energy. You have to keep in mind that these forms of energy are actually the idea created in our mind. It is our mind which manages and structures energy in what we perceive.

Self healing is the ability to circulate this energy in order to improve your physical self. When it is used to heal others, one can become the healer.

Why Vibrational Energy Healing?

This energy is widespread around the body. Sometimes, your senses create blockages in the energy and prevent the energy to flow freely. This disruption can occur in your body as diseases and ailments. They can cause problems in spiritual, emotional and mental self. It causes severe damage to the body when it remains untreated for a long time. One thing you should note that we all are energy beings and the cause of all the issues are energy problems.

Knowingly and unknowingly, you are always influencing others and yourself through your vibrational energy or bio energy in your daily life. When the interaction between you and other person is positive and peaceful, you can gain positive vibes. Likewise, you harness toxic energy when the situation is stressful.

The negative energy causes stress in your body and mind. It can be received from the person who is negative. It may also be caused because of energy blockages. All in all, you have to ensure that the energy fields are flowing freely and are uninterrupted.

You can feel happy and peaceful as long as the vibrational energy flows without any interruption. Avoid going into depression when you feel obstruction in this life force. Instead, try vibrational energy healing to remove the blockage, fix the flow of vibration and restore the life force.

Essential Energy Healing

Essential Energy Healing or EEH is based on helping people restore their pleasure and relax in life. It is actually a spa based in Canada. It offers all the services and holistic treatments to the people to live a healthy life. It takes care of the overall wellbeing and improves the condition of body, mind and soul.

However, this treatment is not limited to only one place. Alternative Energy Healing is getting more popular. It is getting widely accepted and absorbed by the field known as Complementary & Alternative Medicine. There are some forms of traditional techniques like Reiki widely used for centuries. Essential Energy Healing is designed by Mary Maddux as a Western form of energy healing.

It combines various healing methods and two particular forms - Spiritual Healing and Energy Therapy. It consists of Healing Touch. The results of this technique are much like Reiki. Practitioners use either hands-on or hands-off method to improve the spiritual, psychological, emotional and physical well-being. In both methods, healers have to closely focus on their own energy and the energy of patient.

Other Types of Energy Healing

Essential Energy Healing is just a part of Alternative Energy Healing. There are other healing techniques like Qigong, Yoga, Reiki and Acupressure also the part of subtle healing energy. Some of the common forms of energy healing are –

- Emotional Freedom Techniques (EFT)
- Biofield Energy
- Feldenkreis Work
- Faith Healing
- Polarity Therapy
- Meditation
- Spiritual Healing
- Therapeutic Touch

Essential energy is become a part of huge range of healing programs. Energy healing therapies include different techniques but Essential Energy healing is the modern approach. The best part of Essential Energy is that it relies on traditional healing methods and works under the Complementary & Alternative

Medicine (CAM) method to cure the problems holistically.

Energy healing may be long-distance, hands-on and hands-off process. The Energy Healing techniques work through or with these things to heal the person-

- Chakras
- Meridians or Channels
- Astral layer
- Vibrational Energy bodies
- Various Spiritual Layers

Energy Healing & Meditation

By sitting in the posture of meditation, we naturally connect with our inner self. While we disconnect ourselves from the materialistic world around us, both our mind and body are free of all the distractions. Then we set ourselves free to channelize the energy throughout the body.

So, all you need to sit quietly and imagine the energy flowing in the body

Spirituality

freely. Imagine the energy flowing throughout the body. Keep visualizing it to cover you. Stay focused for around 15 minutes. And then slowly get back to the reality. Set a time every day to perform this inner meditation. This process can help you to stay healthy and keep your mind, body and soul on peace. Feel the energy flowing through the body. This process shows the deep connection between meditation and energy healing.

Chapter 6 - Spirituality In Grief

Do sorrow and grief overpower you? Is your loved one died? Are you separated with your spouse? Are you facing the trauma of abortion? Have you lost your job or something that matters most to you, like your home, relationship or health? No matter how traumatic your pain is, there is a supreme power that will help you find hope and heal your broken heart.

Understanding Grieving Process

Understanding how grief works can be helpful to deal with loss. Grief is a healthy, natural process with which we all improve from extreme emotional wounds. All in all, grief is medicine in itself. If you have lost someone you loved the most, you may heard people saying, "Don't lose your heart! He or she is in heaven." It may be true. But you have to learn to deal with the extreme pain of loss. Don't feel guilty if you are grieving because it is the important part of healing.

The process of grieving is mostly like sailing over a sea of storms. In the very first step of having a great loss, the storm of emotions attacks us. We get covered by the heavy layers of suffering and darkness. The weeping winds of sorrow easily wipe away the comforting words. We feel out of control and lonely when we are suddenly swept to the new path of life. There are 4 phases of God's pathway to grief –

- **Shock** – After a disastrous loss of someone, some of the common feelings like unreality and numbness may trap you as nightmare for a few days and weeks.
- **Reality** – When loss takes hold, you experience the deep sorrow, accompanied by various kinds of emotional release like weeping. It may also cause depression and loneliness

according to how much you loved him/her.

- **Response** – The feelings of helplessness and abandonment brings anger, which may be directed to friends, family, God, doctors, and even the person who deserted us or died. Some common feelings are lack of interest, lethargy and guilt on unresolved personal problems or failures.
- **Recovery** – This is something unnoticeable, gradual return to your normal condition. It is the time when you start adjusting to the new situations in life.

For each person, the above phases may vary. So, it doesn't make sense to impose a schedule on anyone. Some people may recover within few weeks or months, while some take several years. Especially within the first year of loss, anniversaries, holidays and birthdays may trigger sudden or deep pain.

Healing a broken heart is just like healing physical injury, like broken leg. So, don't rush the process because it can deter your prolonged recovery. It is like removing the cast sooner than letting the bone solid enough to hold weight. Unresolved grief can cause alcoholism, depression, drug abuse, or various critical problems.

Dealing With Grief

Grief can badly affect our behavior, thinking, relationships, emotions and health. Grieving person may feel exhaustion, sleeplessness, lack of interest, indigestion, or even memory loss. Keep in mind that they are common reactions which can be controlled by joining a prayer group, talking to friends or seeking help of a Christian counselor.

For a grieving person, adapting the new environment, without the person who moved away or died, is the most challenging thing to do. When it is good time to make lifestyle changes, put loved one's belongings away or make new relationships? The answer will be found by learning these recovery processes –

- **Grieve** – Though grief feels bitter, we have to let the sorrow flow through in its natural way. Sorrows occur until we are alive. But we have to get acquainted with grief. If we repress or deny the pain, we will have emotional hardships.
- **Believe** – We have to believe in god's promises and trust that he knows what is best for us and he understands us better.
- **Receive** – Our god wants to give us comfort and happiness but we have to accept it. Proper meditation and prayer can find a place in his presence. He will give us the direction as a father.

Spirituality

Some Common Things You Shouldn't Say to a Grieving Person

Everything around us is torn apart when someone dies who is close to you. And you feel as fragile as a very soft tissue paper. You will feel that a small breeze can shred you totally. Friends may want to console you but most of them are wondering what to say.

They wonder "What If I say something stupid?" or "What if I blurt out the thing that hurts him or her?" Before experiencing grief, I tell you that I was also have no words. By considering both sides, I am suggesting you what to avoid saying to a grieving friend.

1. **Cheer Up! He (Person who died) wouldn't like if you are sad for longer."**
After the death of my father, relatives told me that he would not like if I keep crying. And I should stop crying to

honor his memory. It seems true that because there is no single time when he likes me to see me in sorrow. Though he wanted me to be happy, but I couldn't do that after his death. If you love them deeply, you actually grieve deeply. To reach the other part of grief, you need to be sad if you are grieving.

2. He is in Heaven Now

Of course, heaven is known to be very beautiful. To be honest, I have a problem. I don't want him to be there because he can never be here again. You may call me selfish! I want him here. Not just me. Everyone who lost loved one wants them to be here. I want him here offering advice, teaching me life lessons, singing with me and anything he can do. Though it is sure that I will meet him in Heaven, but sadly I have to die first. And I must say, this thought blows me out.

3. Focus on all the Good Things in Life

Are you serious? As a grieving person, I will definitely not want to hear such words when everything has been shattered behind me. No matter how much this sentence seems "Optimistic". It means I have to focus on all the positives rather than the negatives. Even though I try to embrace the positive parts of life, it never changes the truth that I am suffering from a huge loss. So, a newly grieving person will certainly not feel like he is shouting from the top, "How Lucky Am I!"

4. It's been a long time since he died. Now you should get over it.

When you are grieving, weeks and months no longer matter for you. You never notice how easily weeks and years have been passed. This is how grief works. You may calculate the amount of time since your loved one died. But for healing your broken heart, time doesn't matter. Putting a schedule or timetable on grief doesn't make sense. To be frank, if you couldn't understand that point, it is sure that you haven't mourned the loss of loved one yet. If you have experienced grief in your life, you will feel how disappointing it seems when someone comes to you and suggests you to hurry up and move on.

5. Appreciate all the Pleasant Memories because they will give you peace.

This statement seems to be true. It is something that every grieving person expects to hear. When their mind is whirling, heart is hurting and faith is broken, embracing old memories can give you relief. It is the only thing that helps you create new memories.

6. Control yourself because you have to support your siblings and mom.

When grief is in initial stage, it is as emotionally severe as getting a major surgery. A newly grieving person is fragile and has to heal. After having a surgery, doctors recommend patients to take rest and focus on themselves. Nobody wants him to jump off the bed after having a heart surgery because he has to be in office. So please, stop making them feel even worse by saying that he is focusing on his grief, not his dependents. It is really offensive.

Grief affects each aspect of emotional and physical wellbeing of the person. It hinders the ability to eat, sleep, work and focus. So, never ever ask someone to swallow his sorrow just to focus on his family. It prolongs his grief. The person needs to help himself first, so that he can help others. It is something like rule of using oxygen mask in flights. Here, you ensure proper oxygen for yourself first before helping the people around you.

7. So, How about the movie?

Though you want to do a favor to the griever by diverting the conversations at a light way, a griever wants someone who can help them be real and say something about the hard thing. I mean that sad stuff or human stuff. They expect you to sit and listen to them or even mourn with them. It doesn't mean discussing weather or sport is an offence. Just remember that the actual healing comes from something heavier.

What You Should Say To A Grieving Person?

When your loved one dies, you get a great deal of support and advice. Some suggestions may be helpful, some not. Recently, we have discussed some of the worst statements you should avoid saying to the person in grief. Now, it's time to discuss what to say to the person who is grieving.

1. I Understand How You are Feeling Now

This is not something like "I know how it feels when you lose someone". I avoid uttering this thing for the person who is in grief. If I have never shared same situations with them, how would I know his pain? Circumstances of everyone are their own. Instead, you can say "I feel your pain" which expresses empathy. You can utter these four powerful words to the person in grief. This single sentence can break down all the walls of isolation which is made with regret and deep sorrow. If you merge these words with an embrace or touch, it can lift up their downcast eyes. You may tell him that he is not the one who is grieving.

2. Can I Give You a Hug?

When I was grieving, I was in need for hug. I don't think everyone has same kind of feeling. I was starved for hug. I wanted to hug everyone who is close to me. I wanted to hug even a little pet of my neighbor. I was like a doll which had been broken and every hug worked as glue to get me back to normal state.

3. I'm sorry for all these happened to you

It shows you care and gets to the point. These words feel direct and honest. You can follow two simple but very useful healing steps is to show up your empathy and say "I am sorry to hear that."

4. I am always here for you.

It is true that grief makes everyone uncomfortable. It is really difficult to see someone you know and care about is shattered emotionally. And you may definitely want to support them but it is not so easy. All you need to be there for them and help them in all possible ways. It is one of the most helpful things you should do with them.

5. Do something special for the grieving person

Here, you may offer to do something special for them, rather than uttering a common phrase, "Tell me if you need anything". People are likely to make this kind of gesture as they want to support but they don't know what the person needs. For the newly grieving, the fact is that they really don't know what they need. It may be because they are not ready to figure out. So, it is better to

Spirituality

provide a specific offer. For example, "I am at the grocery store. I will bring you some bread and milk if you like."

6. Are you okay to talk about him (loved one who died)?

When it comes to talk about the person who died, it is obvious that you may worry. There are chances that you may make him sad. But it is not true. When someone loses the person who was very close, they will keep on thinking about the person. The griever is surprised to see how rarely their friends or relatives discuss about the person who died, after several months. It is really heartbreaking. So, if you share a memory about the person who died and bring up his story, it makes the griever feels that you too remember him and it is very comforting for him.

7. Say Nothing

It doesn't mean you should avoid the grieving person or pretend that you don't know about their loss. This kind of attitude would really hurt them. Offer them a hankie and hold their hand. Make some coffee. Ask them to go for a walk. Let them talk whatever they want. It is definitely the biggest gift you can give to a grieving person. Allow them to speak freely.

Managing Grief Through Grief Counseling

Grieving and dealing with loss is really very painful. You may be wondering what are you experiencing and feeling is normal. While facing the loss of someone, some emotions like denial, shock, trauma, anger, sadness, fear and depression can disrupt your strength. With loss of someone, these feelings may disrupt your personal life and they are both overwhelming and powerful. This way, grief counseling is the option that can help you in this painful process and go through the harsh reality of losing someone.

Spirituality

Anyone can be afraid that they can never smile or laugh again because grief brings such intense emotions. You may be afraid that you can never repair your damaged life. If you are in the middle of grieving, you may find the way to resolve your grief and see beyond the pain. Don't let your grief to lead you or it will disrupt your thinking and make you believe that you are trapped forever in despair. Though the path to recovery seems to be difficult and long, there is a light when the tunnel ends.

Try to Absorb the Grief's Impact

When someone you love dies, or you face other kind of loss, it is wise to figure out what to expect. When grief is in initial stage, it is common that you are cushioned from the painful reality due to emotional shock. That feeling of separation is physiological response so you can have enough time to accept the impact of loss on your own way. Our brain and body takes care of us, even though we cannot. The loss of losing someone is so devastating that we may emotionally "turn off" for some time. Hence, we have time to accept the reality and get ready for more challenging times to come.

When the shock collapses, you may experience the difficulty in believing what has happened. You need time to sort through the feelings and thoughts streaming in your mind. You may experience anger, fear, sadness and other powerful emotions.

When It is Important to Consult Grief Counselor?

Almost all of us who grieves face depression at some part of time. If you are depressed, or you are in a phase where you have lost the purpose to live, you cannot do the basic things in daily life. For example, sleeping not enough or too much, taking care of your own hygiene, or having suicidal thoughts. If you have one of such problems, you should consult grief counselor and psychiatrist who can assess your psychological problems and quickly take action to keep you safe and help you heal.

It is important to find the grief counselor and psychiatrist who are well trained to help fulfill the unique needs of the grieving person. It is true that psychologists and social workers cannot prescribe antidepressants. But they can, at least, recommend you some qualified and experienced psychiatrists if they feel that you need medical help for your recovery and safety. If you have undergone the grief and mourning and faced severe depression which caused suicidal thoughts, you cannot handle it on yourself. You need immediate medical help from the professional who can assess the intensity of depression and what's the right time to make you feel safe again.

When we are in grief, we may sometimes be able to move forward due to fear, anger or other emotions. If these emotions are causing trouble for you, you cannot reach the goal of resolution and recovery. Though your life cannot get back to its normal state as it was before such a huge loss, your life still has some pleasure and meaning. You can recover with the help of a grief counselor to move through the process of grief.

How to Find the Best Grief Counselor?

You may contact the hospital near you. Hospitals are always helpful for those who are looking for grief support. It would be better if you can contact the hospital where someone you loved died. The medical social worker in the hospital will ask if you talk to the grief counselor. Most hospitals provide support and helpful resources to the grievers. You may occasionally visit some of the grief counselors until you find the right practitioner. If you are having problem dealing with loss, grief counseling is very important support.

Spirituality

You may find yourself desperately alone due to grief. It feels like you are drifting on the ocean of despair without any hope of finding the shore. It leads to intense emotions. But grief also brings a raft to help you cross the sea of despair and reach the destination. Expert opinion is very helpful because they specialize in fulfilling the unique needs of grievers and you can find the safe haven with their help. There is no need to face the grief alone.

Chapter 7 - How Spirituality Helps Recover From Addiction And Substance Abuse?

When research has been evolved on addiction over the years, it is found that addiction affects our mind, body and spirit. Since treatment tools are based on physical, psychological and social needs, spirituality has played an important role to help people in recovering from addiction.

There is a deep connection between spirituality and addiction and some oldest recovery programs in the world use spiritually-oriented actions like prayer, meditation, personal searching and conscious contact with higher power. According to the National Center on Substance Abuse and Addiction at Columbia University,

- Adolescents and adults who visit religious services on regular basis are

Spirituality

less likely to use tobacco, alcohol or illicit drugs
- Over 80% of Americans believe in some higher power like God.
- Teenagers who are not engaged in any religious services have four times higher risk of getting addicted to illicit drugs and 3 times higher risk of alcoholism than those young people who attend services regularly
- Adults who are not engaged in religious services have 5 times higher risk of getting addicted to illicit drugs and 7 times higher risk of alcoholism than those who visit services regularly.

How Spirituality Cures Addiction & Substance Abuse?

Most people who have been recovered from addiction credit their improved health to spirituality. Even most scientific researches proved that spirituality works wonder in addiction recovery. It leads to the growth of several tools which are helpful in spiritual action and reflection. The National Institute on Alcoholism and Alcohol Abuse initiated a program, Project MATCH which conducted a research. According to the research, the addiction treatment programs based on spirituality have around 10% higher self-discipline rates as compared to other treatment methods. In other studies, an opposite relationship has been found between substance dependence and religious involvement, and between substance use and meditation practices.

Most of the scientific evidences have proved the benefits of Christian addiction treatment, spirituality and Catholic addiction treatment and their growing popularity is no longer a surprise. Spirituality has been incorporated with physical, psychological, and social variables to deliver complete treatment.

The Role of Spirituality in Substance Abuse and Addiction Treatment

Over 87% of Americans introduce themselves as religious and 83% are Christian. With this majority, it is not hard to say that religion and spirituality can help very much in recovery and treatment. Though spirituality is defined to be related to the spirit of someone, relating it to the religious beliefs or religion or pertaining to soul or god, spirituality is perceived subjectively and differently by different person. Actually, spirituality provides meaning and purpose to a person's life.

The best thing is that spirituality doesn't act same to everyone's life. Spirituality may be non-theistic, theistic, based on faith in god, or on ideas of various moral values or inner strength. Spiritually may be based on different religious beliefs. It also represents a non-denominational, broader sense of belief in the spiritual self. You don't have to believe in higher power or attend the church to be spiritual.

For some people, spirituality is just defined with the actual experience of –
- Complete clarity
- Improved awareness
- Authenticity
- Feeling of empathy and understanding
- Higher sense of purpose and meaning

Despite the lack of explanation of spirituality, it is possible that it incorporates treatments and therapies of anxiety and depression. Several studies have found the relationship between religious devotion and spirituality with the ability to deal with depression and stress.

The Origin of Spirituality Based Treatment

The role of substance abuse treatment and spiritually dates back to 18th century in the US. It was the time when Native American religious and cultural movements started spirituality to cure alcohol addiction. In the mid of 18th century, 6 people who were addicted to alcohol wished to recover from it and support one another. So, they established the Washington Society.

Later on, they were transformed into a huge movement which relates their approaches on faith in god. In the 1900s, therapists incorporated religious theology into recovery and treatment approaches with Courtenay Baylor and Richard Peabody. They initiated Lay Therapy Movement and paved the way to establish the world-renowned treatment program, Alcoholics Anonymous, which is based on spirituality.

How Alcoholics Anonymous Helps in Alcoholism Recovery?

Alcoholics Anonymous was one of the first well known recovery programs that incorporate spirituality with addiction recovery and treatment. They smartly link spiritual elements to addiction recovery with mental and physical aspects. The programs emphasize these aspects –

- Reevaluating and exploring the purpose of life
- Trusting and believing in the higher power
- Considering addiction as the mental, spiritual, social and physical symptom
- Committing to ethical and moral behavior
- Developing hope to cope up with addiction
- Admitting wrongs to others, oneself and God
- Using meditation and prayer to connect with God

Spirituality

Benefits of Spiritual Recovery Programs

Basically, counseling is the service where an expert provides advice and guidance to a group or individual. Spiritual counseling is a service where advice or guidance provided is based on spiritual rules. Spiritual counseling benefits heart, mind and spirit. Clients suffering from mental problems like anxiety, depression, bipolar disorder and alcohol or drug addiction can also benefit from spiritual counseling. It helps clients to improve and make lifestyle changes. It provides required guidance and assistance to find out any obstacles ahead.

In Spiritual Counseling, the experts determine their level of interest and the benefits they may get from these programs. In the initial assessment, the treatment options and personal problems are discussed. A typical spiritual counseling program includes the power of acceptance, mindfulness, cultivation of

gratitude and lots more. It teaches you these qualities –
- Staying in the present moment
- Taking responsibility for their own behavior, emotions and related actions
- Exploring the higher power
- Prayer

According to the spiritual counseling experts, the relation between a person and God can provide lots of benefits. A person can grow and achieve most of the milestones in life that they've previously thought impossible.

Spiritual Counseling is helpful for people to accomplish their goals by implementing the idea and accepting that there is a higher force with them. By accepting this, the person believes that they can achieve more success in life.

How Religion Keeps Teen Away from Substance Abuse?

Risk of substance abuse and illicit drug addiction was found lower among teens who were involved in religious practices. Over 63% of religiously active teens gained huge knowledge about the risks and complications due to drug abuse. On the flip side, only 41% of the teens who were not involved in religious practices knew the risk of drug abuse.

According to the research on teens, the early intervention of 12-step programs based on spirituality improved their lifestyle and treatment response. Other studies also suggest that these 12-step programs also helped in providing positive treatment and recovery results with great religious acceptance. Adolescences that hold religious practices, spend time on meditation and attend religious services have less risk of drug abuse. They also have –
- Reduced pain levels

- Lower blood pressure
- Lower cholesterol
- Reduced rate of anxiety and depression
- Shorter or fewer stays in hospital
- More positive and healthy habits
- 29% longer lifespan than average

All such factors prove the important role of spirituality in addiction recovery and treatment. It is the part of holistic approach which helps in recovery of body, spirit and mind.

DISCLAIMER

All Rights Reserved. No part of this publication may be utilized or reproduced in any form, mechanical or electronic, including recording, photocopying, or by any information retrieval or storage system, without written permission from the publisher.

The editor, author and publisher have made their best effort to ensure accuracy in all information in this material. They are not liable for any omissions, errors, or any results related to the use of information in this publication. The author and publisher shall not be responsible for the use of any procedures or steps described.

Copyright © 2015 by Megan Coulter

MORE FROM AUTHOR

The book "**Creative Confidence - Discover Your Unawake Potential & Self-Confidence**" explains the most effective and powerful ways to build a spontaneous self-confidence that lives within us. You will find the ways to bring out your unawake creative confidence that is lying deep inside you.

Creative Confidence: Learn It, Develop It & Change Your Life

Spirituality

A great book, which covers the basic and most important things that proves you can achieve whatever you dream for, just by thinking big. It will teach you principles on using the law of attraction in life. In this book, you will get to know that successful people reach the top only with their beliefs.

The Magic Of Thinking Big: Achieve Whatever You Dream For

In this guide you can learn how mindfulness can make your life better. Practicing mindfulness can make you happier and healthier. Mindfulness is known to systematically control our energy and attention, transform the quality of experience positively and help us realize the humanity at its best.

Mindfulness For Beginners: Live Stress Free Life To Fullest

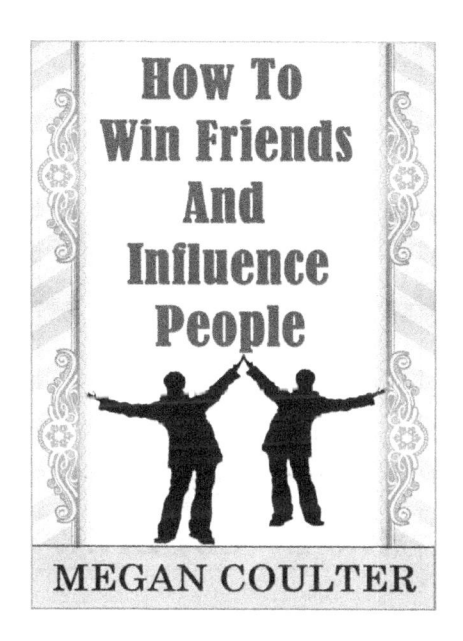

How to Win Friends and Influence People is based on scientifically-proven, amazingly simple principles to influence others. It will teach you how to win friends and influence others to actually like and be ready to implement your ideas, accept your proposals, and buy your services and products.

How To Win Friends And Influence People

Talking is an art, and the one who master the skills of talking can rule the world. You can win the world and people's heart. If you know how to talk properly. Here in this book I am going to share with you what to talk, when to talk, who to talk, where to talk and whom to talk. This book will teach you how important 'talking' is in all spheres of life.

How To Talk To Anyone: Mastering The Art Of Talking

Spirituality

In the book, "**The Power of Introverts**", you are about to know how brains of introverts and extroverts work, and why introverts are underestimated and misunderstood by the extroverted society. In addition, this publication will help you know whether you are an introvert and extrovert and how to use your inner strengths as an introvert.

The Power Of Introverts: Learn To Speak Up Without Raising Volume

The book "**A Curious Minds – Foster Your Creative Potential For Better Life**" introduces you to persistent, restless and unbeatable imagination of children. It shows how a common activity of asking questions can be life-changing for you. This book explains how paying attention before acting can help you in diverse fields and how to make common and repeating tasks more interesting.

A Curious Mind: Foster Your Creative Potential For Better Life

Spirituality

Have you ever come across or heard the word 'codependency?' Well, if you have heard someone tell you or another person "you are codependent" then this eBook is meant for you. You should not only read more about codependency, you should also get to understand many aspects of it that affects us.

Codependent No More: Life Can Be Better When You Overcome Codependency

THE GIFTS OF IMPERFECTION

A Complete Guide To Live Life On Your Own Conditions

MEGAN COULTER

The book "**The Gifts of Imperfection: A Complete Guide to Live Life on Your Own Conditions**" is all about wholehearted living. This book teaches you cultivate the compassion, courage, and connection in your life. "No matter how much you left incomplete and what you have done, you're enough."

The Gifts Of Imperfection: A Complete Guide to Live Life on Your Own Conditions

Spirituality

A lot of people have missed key opportunities in their lives over the years because they failed to see the power of now. Most people fail to live in the now because they prefer to be fear of what they do not know will happen tomorrow. However, this eBook will be able to help you realize why it is important to free yourself from the fear of tomorrow.

The Power Of Now: Practice It And Attain Enlightenment

Here in this book you are going to know about how to make your marriage successful and will also learn about the seven principles that one must follow to make their marriage work. I am sure if you will apply these 7 principles in your married life, then it will be successful and you will lead a happy and healthy life with your partner.

Marriage: Seven Principles of Making Marriage Work

Spirituality

Self-Help Books - The Power Of Now & The Power Of Introverts

MEGAN COULTER

These box set of Self-Help books will give you an introduction to introvert people, their behavior, power of introverts and the power of now. Also it will help you understand how today stands out and why you need to do all you can to benefit from the now.

<u>Self-Help Books - The Power Of Now & The Power Of Introverts: (Power of Now, Power of Introverts, Introvert People, Introverts, Do it Now)</u>

CHARISMA

Increase Your Tremendous Charm and Aura

This book gives you the step by step introduction on charisma, and all about how to control your emotions and to develop charismatic personality.

[Charisma: Increase Your Tremendous Charm and Aura (Charisma Myth, Charismatic Personality, Be Charismatic, Charismatic Leadership)](#)

Spirituality

This book gives you the step by step introduction on how to set Boundaries in each relationship. This book is helpful for both the working professionals and the general readers to set healthy personal boundaries in different relationships, so they can find peace of mind and serenity in their life.

Boundaries In Relationships: Learn When To Say Yes, Make Your Life Healthy, Set Boundaries Between Relationships

Megan Coulter

This book gives you the step by step introduction to Meditation For Beginners, Meditation Techniques, Guided Meditation, Zen Meditation and a lot more!!

Meditation: Complete Guide Meditation For Beginners, Meditation Techniques, Guided Meditation, Zen Meditation

ABOUT AUTHOR

Hi, Megan Coulter is from London, and is an author profession. She after completing her studies, showed her interest in reading and writing books. She started writing her first book after her graduation and the book was - "Creative Confidence- Learn It, Develp It & Change Your Life", as she is very confident girl, she wants to encourage people and wants to develop inner potential in them. The book is very interesting and really helps in developing confidence and motivating people. After that she writes her other books as well on Self-Help for encouraging and motivating people. You can read them on your Kindle devices. Few of them which are well known are The Magic Of Thinking Big, Mindfulness for Beginners, How To Win Friends And Influence People, How To Talk To Anyone, The Power Of Introverts, etc.

Megan is a creative writer and so she chooses her niche in writing creative books, and that really encourages and helps people a lot. Waiting for more books from Megan Coulter??? Keep visiting her page and follow her to get updates.

Facebook:
https://www.facebook.com/pages/Megan-Coulter/853427661394434

Twitter:
https://twitter.com/MeganH_Coulter

Author Central Page:
http://www.amazon.com/-/e/B00VEA8QOW

Made in United States
Orlando, FL
27 March 2024